TURNING THE SCREEN

TURNING THE SCREEN

personalisation and privacy

R&D Griffith-Jones
David Huw Griffith-Jones
Robert James Griffith-Jones

ISBN-13: 9781532702068
ISBN-10: 153270206X

To Grandparents.

As a thirteen year old boy we had monthly lessons at school on how to be good citizens. Each was to teach us something about the world and how we should behave in it. One week it was about debt. There was the usual financial prudence talk and then, in walked, "The Bag Man". And the Bag Man was there to scare us. He'd come to explain just how easily he could, "get to us".

It was 1995. The internet hadn't taken off, or at least, neither the Bag Man nor any kids in the room knew much about it. The talk itself didn't make me scared of getting into debt; the student loans thrust upon my generation a few years later saw to that! But it did impress on me the power of personal information; and this was the Bag Man's currency. Whilst waiting outside your school, he would observe who you talked to and then engage with these same people himself. He'd harmlessly ask where you'd gone, establish the name of your sister to gain the confidence of other interviewees or find out your class so he might speak to your teacher. The uncompromising Bag

Man would even go through your bins to gather every piece of personal information available. Within 48 hours, he proudly claimed, he'd have all the leverage he needed to get the money from you.

Today, all of the Bag Man's conniving leg work can be done in a few clicks.

My day jobs have been to protect individuals' rights and to help Brands to personalise their digital experiences. However, this isn't a marketing book. Nor is it a legal text to help people protect themselves or lobby for legislation. All this information changes year to year, month to month. This is a book, not a slide deck or a website. It is a retrospective of where we have got to and what might come next in personalisation and privacy. Where Google know everything about me, where Whatsapp know my family, Instagram know where I've been and Amazon know what I'm going to buy before I do.

When I was younger, I had a pseudonym on Facebook: Flynn Flinderson. Later, I realised they knew my face, they knew what I had read, they knew what I had watched, what I'd bought, where I'd been, what I had written and who to. My name - it didn't really matter.

David Griffith-Jones, @digitaldavidj

Introduction – The Current Landscape

So you have probably heard about 'Big Data' - the collection of masses of information about each and every one of us. In isolation, each piece of information isn't worth much. However, when combined with other data and interpreted in the right way, it allows for some very interesting, accurate assumptions to be made. Assumptions about you: what makes you tick and what turns you off. In this digital world, companies know how to approach you and where to tickle your impulse to buy or subscribe. Not surprisingly, such knowledge is worth an enormous amount of money. Business success is best achieved through personalisation and it's happening to all of us on a daily basis. If you knew that, you are one of the few who do.

The development of personalisation is nothing less than incredible: it is a completely new way for humans to interact. The idea of meeting a stranger, in the sense you know nothing about that person, no longer applies.

If you're reading this book, we can assume you knew a pre-personalised, pre-digital world. (If you don't then that makes you less than sixteen years of age; may we commend your interest and say "you'll go far, kid".) So, there was this time, not so long ago, when John Doe in the US and John Smith in the UK would see the same page at Nike.com. This wasn't because they were the same anonymous user that any non-profiled persona went under. That would've been impossible: none of us were profiled! Back then, websites served the same content to all users. They were a publication like all others printed before it; crafted and shared in publishing cycles.

Doesn't this seem a peculiar waste? Charmingly quaint? Well, the difference between that time and this is: personalisation. It has caused a landslide shift in the way we are engaged online. The data that has fuelled it is set to flow at even faster rates into the hands of those able to mine it. As the Internet of Things (IoT) takes off in the coming years, whether you have sugar in your coffee or park your car manually will decide how you're greeted in-store; both on the web and in the bricks and mortar shop... by the friendly robot man.

However, this book is not fixated on imagined thoughts of the future. Despite being in its infancy, the art of personalisation is already an incredibly impressive communications tool. After all, it allows us to create a picture of, and provide a personal service to, each of the 3 billion people who visit the world's largest market place. This could, perhaps should, amaze, excite and worry you.

It is natural in a capitalist world that when lucrative opportunities arise they are looted. There was a certain Wild West frontier to the establishment of the internet giants. Google snapped up YouTube pirated content and all. Buzzfeed said hell to copyright as it morphed into the format that allows most usage of other people's content - news. Facebook asked people to list their friends and all the things they like. And so, we have seen that those who took a chance and did it well: made a fortune. Personal data collection was rarely the primary aim of these ventures. Yet in the last 5 years data analysis has boomed and, on the large part, consumers either like it or don't seem to care. Whole industries have grown to gather, process, interpret and leverage information about us.

We're currently in the middle, perhaps merely the beginning, of an apparently never ending explosion of data, consisting of: the cloud, behavioural data, geolocation data and soon many more categories. Sensing money, a handful of large corporates have land grabbed a huge amount of this personal data and established seemingly unassailable positions. All the while the fox is watching the hen house – we are the hens, by the way - with regulation that has failed to keep up with technology or put the public first. Bear in mind, the only bodies capable of regulating data usage are the internet giants, governments or "big business"; and it's in none of these parties' interests to make their data dependant lives more difficult. The public's general awareness is, helpfully, low. Most people are not aware of the data they are dropping nor how it's being used.

Attitudes and policies to the collection and use of our data vary greatly across demographics and countries. As always, knowledge is a key factor too. When it comes to digital privacy the over 60's tend to be more wary; but technologically naive. Whereas, the under 25's tend to be tech savvy but seemingly willing to relinquish control of their personal information. This combination has left a gap which organisations and business have used to great effect.

However, you can't underestimate the instinctive sense of privacy that rests in most of us; nor the value we attach to it. The interplay between personalisation and privacy is considered throughout the book as well as consumer attitudes which should, in theory, be hugely influential to both.

Personalisation? *Talk to me*

Y ou know how investors like something to be summarized for them in a sentence? There's that stuttered pressure of capturing something in a sentence:

> *"Personalisation is serving tailored digital experiences based on known or assumed characteristics of a user".*

It's just far more interesting than that. Personalisation can be so many things it's like saying "wildlife is animals". This needs some explaining.

In fact, the founding principle behind personalisation is nothing new. Its non-digital practice had been adopted since humans learned to manipulate each other a long, long time ago BC. In fact, personalisation will not even be unique to humans on planet Earth. Understanding the intended recipient of a message and adapting its content and delivery accordingly will improve the chances of success, whatever that may be. And so, whether you want to sell a tablet computer or be permitted space to dine on a fresh kill: knowing your audience helps.

In terms of commerce, the provision of a "personal" service has been a long standing ambition for businesses everywhere since the dawn of trade. It must be one of the most commonly used adjectives to describe a company's approach to their work. The reason is consumers, all of them, enjoy experiences that appeal to their own character and predispositions. Even if this means that some don't want to be referred to by name or asked about holidays, thus making the personalised message - as impersonal as possible!

So personalisation is a new name for an ancient, digitally modified principle. It's what is possible in this digital age that is revolutionary, rather than the practice itself. There has been such a transformation in our capability to be personal that we simply needed a name for it and, well, "personalisation" was hard to beat.

PERSONALISATION IN PRACTICE

Websites can welcome thousands of visitors daily. Each of them will have a different reason for visiting the website and be at a different stage of the customer lifecycle; some are coming across a brand for the first time, others are researching a specific purchase and, a few are online to buy right now. As well as coming to the site with different needs and desires, the users will also have distinguishing tastes and exhibit contrasting behavioural preferences. For example, some visitors respond best to an offer of a percentage discount; whereas others are enticed by multi-product deals. Whilst you may find a pop up message frustrating; others respond well to aggressive messaging. Knowing what to say, how to say it, where and when can nurture relationships between a business and its audience. So why not do it?

Companies like banks, supermarkets, telcos and airlines have had deep and rich data for a while - it is only recently they've had the technology, processes and people in place to make this data meaningful and actionable. Now, even smaller entities - who don't habitually collect personal data - can buy or leverage personal information to help construct persuasive propositions.

MORE THAN A NAME AND ADDRESS

The recent explosion in data creation has seen the total data held by businesses double every 18 months. Given that all of us create new data daily, hourly, even minutely it can't be a surprise: we found a voice, they listened. "They" being businesses who base decisions on our varied data, as well as those who sell it to them. We are well beyond the traditional data sets found in a CRM of ten years ago: name, address, payment details, purchase, email address. Nowadays, it can be far more interesting (or should we say personal?), if you're willing to pay for it.

Businesses can access exceptionally rich third party data from the likes of Facebook and Google. Web analytics tools capture locations, frequency of visits, what pages were viewed, where traffic has come from, the device used and much more. Along with multiple other sources of data, this information can be used to form a rich picture of an individual. By analysing the data and developing insights, businesses can identify distinguishing characteristics amongst their user base and segment them accordingly.

IF DATA MINING EXPOSES THE OPPORTUNITY, DIGITAL TECHNOLOGY AND CONTENT PROVIDE THE OPPORTUNITY TO EXPLOIT IT.

When we talk of digital experiences, most of the time we are referring to a user's engagement with websites or apps. However, personalisation need not stop there. Brands are increasingly able to create digital experiences on almost every screen in our lives, with screens popping up in ever more places. Retailers are merging their digital and bricks-and-mortar presences to infuse a physical shopping experience with digital elements. Kiosks, smartwatches, VR, connected cars, big screens, the IoT - these are all platforms where brands are able to create personalised digital experiences. Whether it is a micro-site for a smartwatch or a campaign on a huge stadium screen, there are three things that power all personalisation: data, technology and content. Successful personalisation relies on getting all three working together.

IF IT IS DIGITAL, IT CAN BE PERSONALISED.

Personalisation can be used on any digital asset from apps or kiosks through to emails and websites. It is primarily used to serve targeted content: showing different wording, imagery, prices or offers. It can also be used to deliver differentiated user experiences. A site could have a different structure, navigation, look, feel, flow or calls to action depending upon a user's preferences. The extent of digital tailoring for a specific person or group depends upon what changes will most effectively persuade that target audience.

Here are some of the most common types of personalisation seen today:

• Targeted emails
  "Email" and "marketing", if said together, would prompt looks of distaste when the new darling, social media, emerged in the mid-noughties. However, electronic direct marketing has survived the snobbery and remains one of the most effective ways of communicating with customers. Emails are also one of the easiest and advanced digital platforms when it comes to personalisation.

  Since a personally addressed email doesn't impress today's user like it once might; the power now sits within segmenting email databases. This could be based on information gleaned at the time of sign-up: explicit data either volunteered or required by the user. Alternatively, there's the implicit information leveraged by making assumptions based on the web page that a user signed up from or browsing behaviour following email sends.

  Example: An airline sees that Mrs Inbox has a tendency to click on offers about European city breaks. The next email she receives is about Rome and, when she visits the site, its offers are based on Mediterranean getaways.

- Customisable Apps

  Mobile apps are often better than web experiences for specific and regular tasks, like checking transport information and banking. Because the app sits on a mobile device rather than a web browser it integrates more easily with the device's content and functionality such as notifications, other apps or contacts. A good app can feel personal when making tasks seamless.

  Apps can also provide extremely rich personalised experiences. The interface can be personalised to allow specific common actions to be accessed quicker. Content that is pulled through to the app can be "pre-curated" allowing users to define which content they receive. With the app's geolocation capability users might define locations such as "home" and "work" in order to trigger certain actions or pre-select information and filters. Notifications can be predefined for a wide array of actions and be delivered through distinctive sound or screen alerts.

  Example: A public transport company has an app that allows Mr Tram to set his home and work location. He can also save his most common journeys which are made accessible via the home screen. The app also knows what time Mr Bus tends to leave the house and sends him a notification if there is disruption to his normal routes.

- Dashboards

  Dashboards are areas of a website or app where users can view "at-a-glance" information about their account. Because users tend to look at specific information or execute regular actions, dashboards are personalised to optimise the experience for that individual. A dashboard can even be designed by the user who enjoys more relevant information.

  Example: Mr Credit logs into his bank's website and clicks on a quick link to his dashboard. By default he sees his latest transactions. He wants to know when his salary has been paid and so adds payments from his employer to the 'receipts' section.

- Personalised Web Experiences

  Key content areas such as landing pages, hero banners and calls to action (CTAs) can be personalised according to a range of information. Traffic arriving from a certain type of website or paid keyword might find homepage content which is more aligned to the messaging that brought them to the site. The products viewed influence banner offers. A return user looking at a product for a second time and assumed to be further down the path to purchase than a first timer is given more direct CTAs or a reduced price.

  Actions on websites can also be used to instigate communications between a brand and its user through new channels. To happen, a user must be logged in to the website allowing the brand to associate user with an email address or telephone number stored in the CRM.

Example: The last three times Mr Finance visited a FTSE share index website he went to the latest financial announcements section. An assumed investor rather than a customer the next time he visits the website there's share price information on the homepage's main section

- Targeted Outbound Advertising
Personalised messaging can be leveraged through outbound advertising as well as on digital assets owned by the brand. Adverts served through Pay Per Click campaigns and social media channels can be targeted to a particular audience segment or demographic criteria. An advert's copy and imagery both optimised to appeal to its target audience.

Example: Acme Retail know that those people most likely to purchase their latest product are: women, aged 40-50, in metropolitan areas who are interested in fashion. Acme target Mrs Catwalk with imagery of a fashionable middle aged woman with a cityscape and in language likely to resonate with her age group.

- Dynamic Forms

  Filling in a form is often the last step in the journey to conversion. Having persuaded a user to click "buy now", businesses need to make forms as smooth and painless as possible to complete the sale. A form can be tailored to ask for outstanding information when, for example, an email address is already known. Drop down boxes or free text are chosen to suit; specific messaging served to guide or prompt someone who's delayed in completing.

  Example: Mr Compulsory is a member at Acme Retail. Whilst signing up he provided his name, address, email and phone number. The form that he uses to contact customer services is dynamic, containing only unknown fields. Mr Optional hasn't provided information and so, although on the same webpage, he's asked for more information.

THE DNA OF PERSONALISATION

There are currently four main data sources by which an experience can be personalised. They are the mechanics of personalisation; the four perring engines:

Behavioural personalisation

Points are assigned for a user's cumulative behaviour; these influence their assigned persona once a threshold has been met. Users ascribed to a persona are served particular content targeted towards that group of people. This has the advantage of changing with the moods, tastes or interests of a user.

Profiled personalisation

Information known about the user, typically held within the CRM, is used to serve specific content to that user or possibly their entire persona group. This type of personalisation often comes closest to involving "personal data" in the legal sense.

Triggered

A single action results in certain content being served. It's an "if this, then that" equation. A trigger might be the fact the user started their journey on a certain landing page or it might be they've clicked on a particular content area. Triggered personalisation is similar to behavioural personalisation but is based on single actions rather than patterns.

User set

The user is explicitly encouraged to personalise their digital experience by setting preferences for their preferred type of content or interface. These preferences are then used to define how and what content is displayed.

We're new to this digital sphere and already a users' behaviour can be monitored in so many ways. Personalisation enables detailed insights obtained to shape future engagement. Unlike the internet frontier giants, where the person ended up being the product, the aims of today's companies are more traditional: to sell people stuff. Or, as they'd put it, to provide a "more relevant" digital experience. It's certainly relevant to buying. We'll give them that.

And that - is why investors, like it in a sentence.

But now you know.

About personalisation; not why investors like it in a sentence.

You don't need us to tell you that investors

(A) like to test knowledge and understanding.
(B) are self-important, impatient arseholes.
(C) are busy and don't need a life story.

Do you see how usefully multi-faced personalisation can be?! You'll have to read the above as you wish: you know who you are. The point is now, anyone with the resources can also know who you are – but how did this happen?

Why now? The Perfect Storm

As with any revolutionary advancement there has been a convergence of related events that together created the perfect storm. In the case of personalisation, we have a storm which, at its core, is formed of data.

BUT DATA IN ITSELF IS NOTHING NEW.

We have had access to data for a long time; we've only just been able to truly exploit it. For years, the big supermarkets, telcos and airlines grappled with how to recognise their customers across all touch points. The data from the loyalty cards and at the till, needed to be linked to what the same person did online. Until recently, brands struggled to maximise the potential of personalisation because of three main capability gaps:

i) managing and interpreting data
    Data had been collected on unconnected legacy systems in different formats. The amount of data collected was vast but data analysis capabilities were lagging. Data needed to be pulled, cleansed, housed and analysed separately. In order to give numbers meaning, a framework

was needed to derive actionable insights. Once all this was done, the feedback loop was long. Too long.

ii) managing personalisation tools

Software that powers personalisation is often show-cased as being manageable by marketers without the need for technical assistance from developers. However, like many claims made by management everywhere, personalisation programs can be labour intensive, require technical expertise and plenty of planning. Time that few businesses could afford; however much sense adopting personalisation made.

iii) managing content production processes

Effective personalisation increased the volume of content required to deliver it. Different personas or scenarios necessitate variable images and copy. All such content needed to be managed in a way that made it easy to update and linked in with the personalisation tool. This requires an increased investment in content and a more structured approach to content production. Personalisation needed to improve to make it commercially viable.

TECHNOLOGY STEPPED UP – AND IN.

Personalised content certainly needed to become easier and more accessible. Once again we waited for technology to step up, and in. Data was linked, insights made and personalised content delivered: all in real time.

Driven by the success of early adopters of personalisation, content delivery platforms capable of serving personalised content were created and refined. The theory had become highly practical. Amongst others, Adobe Target and Sitecore's Experience Platform made it possible for marketers to run a personalisation program without a developer. Non-technical marketers were managing personalisations without relying on code changes. This created the facility to act nimbly and shortened the cycle from data, through insight to implementation.

IBM's Watson – a question answering computer - has over 100 different techniques to analyse a user's natural language, then process, retrieve and reason with incredible amounts of data in real time. Scoring the evidence, merging and ranking hypotheses it produces a precise answer. This is insightful data crunching on an enormous scale, instantaneously.

Content is also better managed today with images used across several platforms stored in one location. Such a structured approach to content production and storage is critical to effective personalisation. Things can get very messy, and quickly. Where four distinct user groups are to be targeted, four different content versions need to be created and served. Without structured content delivery and creation systems feeding neatly into the technology where the digital experience takes place – it's unmanageable, complicated mess.

Many thanks to Tech for sorting it out.

YOU PLAYED YOUR PART

In 2010, Google CEO Erik Schmidt claimed that every two years we create as much data as had been done by the whole of humankind until 2003. The legitimacy of this bold statement has been widely debated. What is a fact, however, is the astronomical increase in data: Google deals with 3.5 billion searches per day and Facebook can attribute its 2.7 billion daily likes and comments to individual users. The tools of giants from San Fran have been engrained into our day-to-day lives. Personalisation has thrived on this new diet of data drops, so rich in their variety: opinions, hopes, fears, where, when, who with.

Whether Erik Schmidt was exaggerating or not: our stuff is everywhere.

And the data spectrum has expanded elsewhere, away from social media. In fact, away from the online world all together. With today 91% of companies (min. 11 employees) using a CRM system to capture offline; so where you shop, what you buy and how you get home is all recorded too.

TECHNOLOGY LEFT THE LAW BEHIND

There is a direct conflict between personalisation and privacy. There is no doubt that the lack of legal regulation has assisted the boom in data collection. And we know now that people behave freely, often too freely, online. Whilst human kind has been gifted this new way to interact and express itself; the law must react to how we will inevitably upset each other with it.

Is it right that our data can be captured and traded? Does the general user know what's happening behind their screen? Let alone consent to it happening. There's clearly a need for protection; the problem is that privacy isn't easily defined and is therefore difficult to enforce. Privacy is a huge reason to "turn the screen". Away from you. So let's talk more about it…

How dare you, that's private! Isn't it?

So humanity has this new stage to perform. Boundaries are still forming and these will necessarily shift. And continue to shift. But privacy, not all that long ago, moved a lot slower. Despite the vast change, the opinion of old rings as true now, as it did then.

In English law the earliest cited definition of "privacy" comes from Judge Cooley in 1888. Rather succinctly he defined privacy as "the right to be left alone". But what does it mean to be left alone today?

The masses of personal information that exist now and the sophisticated, modern means of collecting it could never have been imagined in 1988, let alone 1888. At the time Judge Cooley identified the crux of privacy, snoopers were largely limited to eavesdropping on conversations, rifling through papers or watching from afar. Sophisticated stuff! However, the core behavioural driver behind the right to privacy has remained the same. Our ego and sensitivities have changed very little.

Most people instinctively feel their "right to be left alone". It is a pillar of free society. Those that disagree, you'd have to assume, have reason to exploit it: commercial, criminal or otherwise. With this in mind, what protection does the law offer to you and I from those who conspire to learn everything about us? We appear to have abandoned "the right to be left alone" and made it complicated. And ineffective. Individuals should have security and control over personal information so that it's not unfairly used to influence them in their decisions. Yet this is already happening. On a very large scale.

DEFINING WITH THE TIMES

Privacy has more recently been defined as "a right to be free from secret surveillance and to determine whether, when, how and to whom personal information is revealed". The European Convention on Human Rights chips in by enshrining "a right to respect for private and family life, home and correspondence" which closely mirrors the wording of the UN Covenant on Civil and Political Rights. In 2014 the UN High Commissioner for Human Rights produced a report looking at privacy in the digital age with the purpose of examining "the protection and promotion of the right to privacy in the context of domestic and extraterritorial surveillance and/or interception of digital communications and collection of personal data, including on a mass scale". Quite a mouthful. But clearly, privacy matters. It is a fundamental human right and as the High Commissioner emphasized the infringement of privacy impinges on associated freedoms of expression and association. Though, as a term, the meaning and extent of privacy continue to develop - the core meaning has not changed for centuries.

SO WHAT'S SO DIFFICULT?

Part of the reason why the boundaries of privacy are hard to define - and thus offer us protection - is because "personal information", a key component of the law, has a colloquial meaning which differs from the more specific legal definition. Colloquially, personal information is almost anything that you'd prefer not everyone knew - its knowledge could be embarrassing. This could include what you ate for breakfast, your favourite brand of pants or the fact you snore (only when drunk, so you say). Things that don't, by themselves, identify you as an individual. Such information may be personal between you and I, but not in the law's judgement. Not on paper anyway.

The legal definition of "privacy" is far narrower than our own cringed, red-face test. It varies across jurisdictions and statutory instruments but at its cleanest states that "personal information" is:

"information where a person is identified or could reasonably be identifiable".

The first part is easy to recognise. It is information that clearly identifies an individual - like a name or an email address. The second part is more complicated and includes such information that, when combined with other information, could identify an individual. That favourite word of lawyers also appears, "reasonable". This word always manages to blur the lines and give the law enforcers – courts and regulators - room to interpret and develop the law themselves. Such grey areas can provide the flexibility necessary to deal with a concept that risks out manoeuvring the courts and legislators. However, inevitably, uncertainty comes with it.

Currently, the law requires a realistic chance that someone armed with the latest knowledge and technology could feasibly combine information in order to identify another. Although to theoretically identify them is not enough. In theory, all manner of seemingly innocuous pieces of data could be combined to identify a personal detail about you. And, in any case, technological strides are quickly turning the theoretical into readily available; and it is difficult to predict how independent pieces of data will be interpreted together.

THE MODERN INTERPLAY: PERSONAL AND PRIVATE

People's mobile phones are intimate screens - what else do you use in bed, on the toilet and at your desk? They are powering increasingly personalised experiences by learning the user's preferences and becoming the control centre for all other smart devices. It is a very *personal* device whether or not it falls within the "personal data" definition. There is an almost intimate relationship between a mobile device and its user. When someone is on their own device on a secure private network there is an expectation that the activities constitute a private act. People would certainly be uncomfortable with that information being broadcast or monitored.

It is private without necessarily being "personal information" that is deserving of the law's protection.

So what are the common types of personal information and where are they found? There are the traditional forms of identification a bank might ask for: passport, driving license, utility bills, birth certificates and bank statements. These documents are used as proof of identity. Outside of these core documents: a person's age, salary, property, expenditure, travel details, account numbers, sexual activity, medical health and personal relationship issues are without doubt broadly considered private. Though not always personal; as you can't be personally identified by them.

There's also the digital footprint we leave nowadays: purchases we've made, locations we've been to, activities on fitness apps, websites browsed, Googled, photos we're tagged in and data we've gobbled up. Whilst some of this might be treated as "personal information" and protected by law, very often it's not. Instead it's considered information that by default should stay private. Very often, it doesn't.

CONSENT

The big companies that billions of us engage with on a regular basis have mountains of information about us. Supermarkets know what we eat, telco's know who we communicate with, social networks know who our friends are and then there's Google, who know almost every question on our minds! We freely give away this information – trustingly or naively – when agreeing to websites and apps' terms and requests. We do so, because in exchange these companies provide us with services we want. Our lack of caution you'd assume suggests that it is not what others know about us, it's rather a question of what companies do with the information. That, and naïvity.

WE'VE ALWAYS SHARED AND...

You'd have to say people are generally happy to exchange personal information so long as that information is only used in certain circumstances. This attitude is well established. I'd gladly, if sheepishly, tell a pharmacist personal information in order to get the best medicine. And my Grandfather would've done too, long before this digital age. But neither me, nor my Grandfather, would be pleased to find out that such personal information was later used to sell us an unrelated financial product. People instinctively want to control their data and how it is used. If a company oversteps these instinctive personal boundaries, although they may not fall foul of any privacy laws, the trust of the individual is likely obliterated. This could affect a brand's credibility and ultimately sales. Whilst the law is open to interpretation, a customer's sensibilities are easier to predict.

SO WHERE DO WE GO?

Since technology's rapid advancements blew out the scope and vulnerability of the right to privacy, there has been little open, educated conversation about our approach to the issue. The lucrative rewards available to those who exploit our personal information and the loose definition of "privacy": leave us with a right that is very difficult to protect. And so, companies know and legally share all manner of information about us. The way people feel about this – we'll come to later. But how much knowledge do consumers have?

In truth, very little. Digital is such a new and ever evolving tool, it's been decided that we'll go with the flow. People know how to use the internet but have absolutely no idea what it looks like on the inside. Some know the names of things but couldn't give any kind of real explanation of how our digital toys work. And this is all okay; because there are plenty of things we use that we don't understand. However, other products come with symbols, warnings and instructions. Why not the internet? Because - people wouldn't read it? Well, it would certainly need to be short. A one page infographic? Displayed on all websites and accessed from a badge of honour on the homepage.

That's just an example. The fact is that the law, as it stands, struggles to offer a predictable defence for consumers. So why not make it the law to educate users? Privacy could be regulated by the individuals who venture into the digital space. The human importance of Cooley's "right to be left alone" is clear and we should all be given the visibility to administer it. The right consists of two parts:

i) "Don't watch me" relating to how and what information is collected about individuals.
ii) "Don't bother me" encompassing individuals who are targeted with information known about them.

Looking ahead, laws will need to be established with each new technology and consumer touch point. There will be fresh ways to watch and bother; the right to be left alone will forever be tested. The most flexible approach is to put the power in the hands of the public. Educate and inform users so they know where and when they're being watched. Know what's being looked at and balance this against what they stand to gain. Then - say piss off if they want to.

(Leave me alone just sounds too pathetic. "*Leave me alone, Google*" - they just wouldn't listen).

Tech: No place to hide

People knew that phone calls could be tapped. Some would have known that our emails could be intercepted. But did we ever consider that millions of people like harmless (I assume?) you and I, would actually be spied upon by governments? The Snowden expose has brought privacy into focus and should stimulate a discussion of how technology's power to collect and process data is wielded.

You'd expect that, by now, we would all be concerned about how much of our lives' details are stored on record. Or, more to the point, how easily such personal information can be stolen from those storing it. Barely a month seems to go by without another high profile hack coming to light:

March 2014 US Government Employee database compromised exposing personal details of over 2 million federal employees

August 2014 Apple's iCloud hack leading to publication of thousands of private photographs including naked celebrities

October 2014 Saved Snapchat images are leaked from a third party site

November 2014 Hollywood is rocked by the leak of Sony employees' emails and employment records

February 2015 Uber announce up to 50,000 drivers details were compromised in an attack

March 2015 British Airways Executive Club member database is hacked revealing travel and loyalty points data

April 2015 Facebook phone number harvest allows a hacker to link phone, profile picture and names despite privacy settings

May 2015 eBay's customer accounts are compromised with customers urged to check payment details and passwords

July 2015 Ashley Madison, the private dating site for cheating spouses, is hacked revealing database of users' identities and intimate sexual preferences

August 2015 Carphone Warehouse's 2.5 million customer database is stolen

September 2015 Experian lost the information of 15 million customers in a hack that stole names, addresses, passport, social security and driving license details

November 2015 Toy firm Vtech admitted a hack that allegedly saw 4.8 million customer details stolen, including sensitive information about children and their parents

December 2015 Hyatt has payment data stolen from half of its hotels globally

A long list of some huge and wealthy organisations losing user data. In fairness, it's being stolen. But it's not safe.

So what happens to stolen data? Often it ends up on the murky dark web: mostly used in the £4 billion-plus a year online credit card fraud industry. It can, for example, be used to enhance algorithms to crack security codes, guess passwords or tease information out of victims with personal information. Stolen data can also be useful for blackmail or espionage reasons should the day require it. Once introduced to the dark web, personal information is circulated and copied; becoming increasingly available and searchable.

As tech giants and governments are hacked – and our personal data stolen – with such ease: you could say we're void of any privacy. That supposedly fundamental human right. But then this is illegal activity. The work of criminals is difficult to prevent and clearly they don't care much for human rights! As victims we manage to muster an outpouring of frustration with each breach but don't live in fear of the next hack. Should we be more scared? Perhaps. But then, where have we got to hide?

Beyond exposing the terrifying vulnerability of our data, the frequency and breadth of breaches also highlight the staggering volume of personal data that is being stored by so many corporations, employers and government bodies. As we've discussed, in 2016, regulation is very much behind the curve. And so we are left to leave a huge and valuable, passive digital footprint which is stored, sold, processed and used. Here are some perfectly legal examples of where in the world, privacy no longer exists:

Wifi

Example information available: location, mobile device ID, webpage views, login credentials

A connection to any network that provides the internet could be used to collect everything you send and receive over connected devices. This applies to 4G as much as wifi connections. Your device will also pass information to wifi-routers without even connecting. In 2013 some retail brands started wifi sniffing for MAC addresses in your phone. A MAC address is your phone's unique identifier that is broadcast to every potential wifi router listening. By recording each device that comes into range, the wifi network can log the frequency and duration of a visit. Brands could use this to identify a repeat visitor in store. Matching this with data from the tills they could ascertain far more.

Phone masts

Example information available: location, mobile device ID, billing data

Your device pings masts which can be triangulated to give your location to within 100-200 metres. The legislation on how this data is used varies between countries, but is frequently employed by security services in investigations. It may also be requested for a variety of other purposes. For example, Telco's sell anonymised data to help companies understand rich footfall data at certain locations. This data gives location based demographic, behavioural and financial information to brands who may be wondering where to open a store or target an offer.

Mobile operating systems and apps

Example information available: phone calls, messages, online searches, pincodes, web browsing, GPS location, email, contacts, pictures, audio from microphone, images from camera

The companies behind the Operating System on devices (Apple, Google, Microsoft) receive rich data sets from the device's owner. Almost everything you do on your iPhone could be stored by Apple. This access can also be opened up to apps, most often with the requirement of express consent from users. Location, name, email, friends, pictures, microphone access, camera access - these are standard app permissions. Apple's app store has approval processes which, amongst other factors, are supposed to monitor the validity of permissions being requested by an application. Google's apps don't have such pre-approval; instead they largely rely on the community to police apps for permissions that shouldn't be there.

Social media

Example information available: facial recognition pattern, social connections, locations, browsing habits, demographic information, interests

The richness of data held by Facebook is beyond the wildest dreams of marketers ten years ago. Anyone who's taken the time to read their terms and conditions realises the user signs away almost all rights to content hosted there. Explicit actions, browsing behaviours, social connections, locations and demographic data are all combined to provide brands with a highly targetable collection of identities. Facebook expertly mine and sell data dropped on their site, though their tentacles extend beyond the platform itself.

Any website which has a Facebook widget can be used to capture browsing behaviour to add to your record. So Facebook not only monitor what you do on their app, Instagram and Whatsapp; they can also track what you do outside of the platforms they own. Using a combination of pixels and cookies they're able to match up general online browsing with the platform data they own. Almost any site that encourages you to "like" or "share" will also be sending information back to Facebook.

Browsers

Example information available: archive of websites visited, actions on websites, shopping behaviour, articles read, videos watched, locations

Whilst apps are dominating the mobile experience, browsers are still the most frequented gateway to much of the online world. User data gathered via browsers is predominantly done by cookies. Cookies are small snippets of code that are "dropped" onto a user's browser. They can be used to remember preferred settings, to pre-populate information or to recall previous behaviours, such as visiting a particular page. Our browsers have hundreds of cookies dropped on them, monitoring that browser's behaviour across the internet. Websites also contain code used for tools like web analytics or personalisation engines. By recording browsing activity and engagement with websites, a rich picture can be established of the user. This includes looking at your location, device used, how you came to the site, what buttons you clicked and the pages you looked at.

Special mention

One company knows so much data about us, that its power is enormous: Google. Their Android operating system, Chrome browser, Google Maps, Google Drive and Google Mail as well as their core offering of Search provides them with unparalleled information about people; where we are and what we do. Some might say what we think and how we feel.

So by all means get angry about companies losing our data; criminals pose a real threat to our privacy. However, what we should really be talking about, are the legal ways in which companies observe and record us. Fortunately, it is in a company's own interests to protect its users from theft of their details. They will do all they can to prevent a hack for fear of suffering huge reputational damage. However, the scope and methods they use to harvest data for a commercial advantage – call us cynical - but we shouldn't trust them to protect our interests with quite the same level of diligence.

Attitudes to online privacy are both complex and continually shifting. Demography, tech savviness, geography
as well as personal circumstances and context all alter our
perception of a helpful, personal (or freaky, intrusive) digital
service.

Different brands will naturally receive different permissions from their customers. We expect banks to know
about our financial profile but might be less comfortable
with our supermarket having the same access. An airline
has clear permissions to analyse our travel habits just as
a hotel may our dietary requirements. Ultimately it often
comes down to how useful the granting of access is to the
customer.

What is deemed "useful enough" to share information with
brands will vary from person to person. However, research con-
ducted by Ipsos MORI (2014) found that consumers broadly fit
into three camps:

Privacy Fundamentalist about a quarter of people you know
will be privacy fundamentalists. They vehemently oppose

anyone, doing anything with their personal data. Not unless it is both necessary and explicitly authorised. Brands should watch their step with these guys, damage is easily done.

Privacy Unconcerned one tenth of people have no concerns at all with sharing their data nor how organisations choose to use it. Like digital naturists they walk with nothing to hide, loving everything this digital world has to offer.

Privacy Pragmatist – the majority of people are in this category. Over two thirds of people say they will accept the processing of data so long as it is used to their benefit. Pragmatists are cautious like the Fundamentalists, yet see the fun in stripping off. Just not as much as their Unconcerned cousins. There's an appropriate time and place to reveal yourself.

It will be interesting to see how the membership of each group changes with time. We are, after all, right at the start of this digital venture; whether future generations will view us as frigid or free loving remains to be seen. A lot will depend on the education (or lack of) received by consumers regarding personalisation techniques and the personal information being used to engage them.

The research by Ipsos MORI also identified specific influences on a consumer's attitude to personalisation and privacy. Between this survey and others, current attitudes appear to pivot around the following eight factors:

1) It depends where

   Whilst 69% of Swedes would prefer to keep information and online activities private - even if this meant not getting personalised and relevant experiences - only 24% of Chinese felt the same way.

2) It's none of your business

   Inevitably there are some things that people don't want to disclose: 30% of those surveyed were comfortable with receiving recommendations based on past purchases, however only 17% wanted information about their location to be used.

3) It depends who's asking

   Whereas 32% of those surveyed by IPSOS Mori trusted supermarkets to use information in the right way; only 19% felt the same way about media companies.

4) It depends if you're asking

   The majority of people do not consider the mechanics behind personalisation when presented with it and instead view content at face value. Unless it is announced to them or the content is explicitly personal, many consumers are blind to personalisation actions powered by their personal data.

   This is illustrated by the responses received by Ipsos MORI to the question of: what would make you consider ending your dealings with a company? When prompted to think about data, two of the top three ways a company could poison the relationship related to selling or losing personal data. However, when unprompted, data hardly made people's top ten. Clearly, therefore, data is not naturally at the forefront of customers' minds when they think about their interactions with businesses. Not yet, at least.

5) It's an age thing
Surveys tend to agree that opinions diverge according to age. Older users are likely to be more naive about what companies are doing with their data, which is fortunate for businesses, as they are also less in favour of the personalisation techniques powered by such data. When told exactly what data a company was using to serve personalised content to them: over60s were more likely to be uncomfortable with the idea.

In contrast younger people are more familiar with companies processing their personal information and almost resigned to it happening. There is a sense that they have little control over what companies do with their data and that, even if they tried to protect their privacy, they'd be fighting a losing battle. This age group have grown used to having a curated digital presence on social media and so have an intuition for the public nature of the web. Some openly expect brands to serve them according to preferences as the quid pro quo for them providing or making accessible their personal information.

6) It's convenient, so...

In a 2012 survey by Accenture consumers were asked whether they preferred a personalised web experience based on their behaviour being tracked or, alternatively, a nonpersonalised experience in the absence of tracking. 64% said they preferred the personalised experience. The value to the consumer was that they saw products and received sales messaging that was aligned with their interests. This means a more relevant digital experience that's ultimately more convenient as it saves time searching.

7) It's my call

Whilst almost three quarters of consumers surveyed by Accenture said they preferred doing business with retailers who use personal information to make their shopping experience more relevant; a massive 88% thought companies should give them the flexibility to control how their personal information is used.

8) It's appreciated and always has been

According to a study from the University of Texas there are underlying psychological drivers that mean humans are predisposed to personalised experiences. The two key factors are: our desire for control combined with the discomfort of being overloaded with information.

Remember, the opposite of a personalised experience is a "one size fits all" approach where individuals are not catered for. This means a consumer wading through irrelevant content. Digital personalisation allows users to express their preferences, thus, improving an experience. This sense of control develops an intimacy with each interaction; this has been good for business for a long, long time.

Inevitably, the above attitudes will change; new pivoting factors will develop. At present, most consumers aren't even aware of their browsing behaviour being tracked in the background. A consumer is, however, more likely to notice and therefore resist communications that target them due to personal or private data. To this extent, to avoid fracturing relationships with customers, businesses adopting personalisation should be more conscious of not "bothering" people than "watching" them.

The adage, "what you don't know, won't hurt you" (which, of course, is utter nonsense) could be adapted slightly to "what consumers don't know, won't make them angry". Now this is actually very hard to dispute. If a Corporate Bible existed, this enlightening expression would surely be enshrined in the Ten Corporate

Commandments - it's just so wonderfully disparaging and ruthless. Worryingly, as we've mentioned, consumers currently know very little; meaning the personalisation party swells in this time of blissful consumer ignorance. The minority, Privacy Fundamentalists, can stay at home if they wish. Until a huge scandal reveals some dark truths or consumers are properly educated, the general attitude is one of "more personal please".

References:
Ipsos-mori.com/researchpublications/trendsandfutures/
    PersonalisationvsPrivacy
Accenture.com/AccentureRetailPersonalization-SurveyFact-
    SheetMarch2015
Repositories.lib.utexas.edu/handle/2152/18054

The different degrees of "personal"

When it comes to getting personal with customers, not all brands are born equal. Evidently personalisation is a machine that runs on data and there is a huge disparity between those companies at the top of the data food chain - who put personal interaction with users at the heart of their business model - and companies using personalisation as and when it's needed.

Below we have identified the four categories of businesses according to their access to data and, therefore, personalisation capabilities:

Tier 1 - Tech Giants - companies such as Facebook, Google and Apple. Enormously rich data access means their business models focus on the very ability to be personal with users.

Tier 2 - Blue Chip - airlines, telecommunication companies and supermarkets. Access to behavioural and personal information is often mixed with rich data based on loyalty programs and a sophisticated CRM.

Tier 3 - High Volume - popular retail and media brands. Through their traffic, products or type of content these businesses have a greater opportunity for behavioural personalisation than most.

Tier 4 - The Rest - almost all businesses have access to some personal and behavioural information that can be used for personalisation.

DIFFERENT CAPABILITIES, DIFFERENT APPROACHES

Sitting at the top table are the likes of Facebook, Google and Apple. These companies are personal to their core. Passing through their servers are user locations, their personal information, personal communications, web browsing history and lots more. These companies make money from selling insights, data and access to users: in terms of "data mining" these guys have the biggest drills and heaviest sacks. And although their terms and conditions emphasize a user's ownership of his content, they also grant themselves wide ranging rights to use and monetise it.

And monetise data they do. Extremely well. Being so well-resourced, Tier 1's Tech Giants boast the most cutting edge data, content and technology capabilities. In other words, they have made it their job to excel in the key components necessary for personalisation. The sale of insights and data to other businesses makes up a significant part of their business model. Yet their involvement needn't end there: users can also be targeted on the platforms owned by Tech Giants. Google Adwords and Facebook advertising are two prime examples of this; such platforms allow brands to be highly specific about which customers they target and how they engage with them. It's fair to say, the players in Tier 1 hold all the personalisation cards and, for a fee, they're prepared to share them.

This isn't to say, however, that businesses sitting in Tiers 2 – 4 have no cards of their own. Far from it, they too can play the personalisation game and, some of them, very well too. Often, Tier 2 and Tier 3 companies aspire to having their own joined up data, CRM and content systems that allow for market leading personalisation.

The objective for any company outside of Tier 1 is to successfully combine: data analysis, digital content production, marketing and technology capabilities. This requires both detailed planning and the commitment of significant resources for the ongoing management, analysis and optimisation of communications. Essentially, it's a lot of hard work.

TOO MUCH TO HANDLE

After the initial planning and setup of a personalised digital experience there is still a large amount of analysis and optimisation work required to truly make it hum.

This is an ongoing process and there's always the risk that too much data can lead to information paralysis. Although software is available to make real-time updates, often the subtleties of the market need a human mind to oversee the design, content and development support processes. At present, campaign management tools need to be vastly improved before this can become a simple task.

Then there's the continuous management of the content: ensuring it's optimised for the personalised area of a user interface. This requires both digital design and user experience expertise. Yet more man hours.

And the concerns of businesses extend way beyond resource issues: there are inherent risks associated with the processing of personal data. The two main threats are that the data is compromised or misinterpreted. Consider, for example, the potential harm of personalised messaging targeting an apparently pregnant lady who – unknown to the company – has recently suffered a miscarriage. Equally, some people may be offended if it's evident that they've been labelled as a "blue-collar" worker. Clearly, even when data is stored safely, companies cannot afford to disregard the potential for unintended consequences, even if they're due to a consumer's own irrational behaviour or protectiveness over their privacy.

As costs mount, time lapses and stress levels rise; it's easy to see the appeal of relying on the personalisation power leveraged through the Tech Giants of Tier 1. It must also be remembered that in dealing with this heavy workload, many of the businesses within tiers 2-4 are further hindered by their legacy systems. From their point of view, the Facebooks and Googles offer them a more realisable personalisation goal. So, very often, they're willing to pay for it.

But not always. There is an alternative solution: be less personal.

LESS PERSONAL DOESN'T MEAN LESS EFFECTIVE

Since sophisticated personalisation can require significant investment in respect of data, content and technology capabilities many companies opt for something more akin to "focussed targeting" than "personalisation". Sometimes high-level segmentation, such as looking at the channel that brought a user to the site, can be just as effective as an expensive one-to-one personalised experience. By knowing which link the user came to a website via, or recognising the user's device, an experience can be tailored and made more relevant. Brands don't need to process huge amounts of personal data in order to focus their communication in this way. This lighter touch approach allows companies to start with some of the lower hanging fruit without making a large upfront investment.

Fundamentally, the aim of personalisation is to break an audience into groups that share similar traits. It's a communication that varies according to known or assumed information about the user. This information doesn't even need to be "personal" either in the legal or colloquial sense. Users might be divided into segments, cohorts or personas based on their data scores when assessing:

1. Behavioural need - I want to cook a recipe that takes less than 20 minutes.
2. Demographic type - I am a man aged 30 who lives in London.
3. Historic behaviour - I tend to look at the vegetarian section and compare prices.

Behavioural needs can be derived from the user's preference or search settings. Research into a demographic type might show that there are defining characteristics and preferences within a particular group of users. By analysing patterns of behaviour and interactions, businesses are informed of a user's propensity to take a "next action". For example, if a customer has viewed a particular section of a website and undertaken a specific action – perhaps, adding an item to a wish list - they could be identified as being more likely to make a purchase. The insights derived from each categorisation can drive effective online personalisation.

It is personalisation according to behavioural traits, rather than demographic, that has proven to be most effective and it's a method employed by many of today's businesses. Crucially, it doesn't require any "personal" information in order to be executed as each user can remain entirely anonymous in all respects, apart from one: how they've acted.

There are so many potential personalisation activities it means businesses must ensure they are targeting the best groups in the most effective way. As we've discussed, it is a resource-intensive method of communicating.

So, rather than personalising every part of the journey for every user, a personalised experience tends to focus on key types of users through the most common user journeys. Ultimately, the investment in personalisation must see a return in terms of the business' goals such as increasing sales or customer satisfaction KPIs.

Furthermore, depending upon how a personalised experience is crafted, there will be varying levels of content and technical capabilities required to power that personalisation. For example, a personalisation might require multiple content versions to be created and published across several sections of a digital journey; whereas others need a single instance. All of this weighs into the balance of what personalisation work is prioritised by the business.

We've been outlining the varying degrees to which today's businesses are adopting a personal approach. And so, clearly, this must also include: not personal at all.

A prudent question for a business to ask must be: is the personalisation worth it? Whilst personalisation can undoubtedly have huge benefits for a business there is no point personalising unless the experience is more effective than the standard "one size fits all" broadcast approach.

Sometimes, it's correct to take the easy option – God bless it, in all its simplicity.

Future Personalisation

Woh! The innovation trigger is pulled. Hype resonates around the room; followed by a peak of inflated expectations and then, disappointment.

Personalisation was, according to the 2015 Gartner Hype Cycle, just pulling out of the "trough of disillusionment". This ominous sounding place is the period when a product or concept doesn't live up to earlier, inflated expectations. Lessons must be continually learned by all stakeholders: from those who practice to those who preach. If businesses hone their personalised offering and consumers recognise sufficient benefit to buy-in; we may then see the critical change in behaviour. This might be as dramatic as streaming music, rather than downloading, rather than buying a CD, or far more subtle.

As it is, personalisation is edging onto Gartner's "slope of enlightenment" whereby the true potential of a concept starts to be realised in practical rather than theoretical terms. It is during this time that we tend to see mass adoption. Given the many and varied uses we've already highlighted, to think, all this time we've been hanging around the sorry sounding trough! It puts us at an extremely interesting stage of development with exciting extensions of personalisation to come.

We should not, however, forget that personalisation is more than the technological advancements that define its potential scope and reach. Thus far, personalisation has enabled humans to go to new depths of "personal". And that sounds a little creepy, right? Which is exactly the point. Technology alone will change nothing, it is the attitude and behavioural changes that may, or may not, follow which give rise to a transformation. This is the difficulty in predicting the future! The knowledge and interest of consumer's five years from now is a total mystery.

WHAT WE CAN (KIND OF) SAFELY SAY

The as yet unknown attitudes and behaviours will surely mould personalisation's future by influencing the type of executions that brands feel are worth undertaking. First and foremost, we'd expect the biggest influencer to be the wider attitude to privacy and its never-ending battle, on a legislative level, to regulate personalisation.

Behavioural changes will also spawn new technologies. The impact of new technologies on personalisation is two-fold; they could just as easily close opportunities for personalisation as make them more bountiful. For instance, it's difficult to imagine our data security worries ever subsiding. Such fears might mean consumers start paying a premium for their information to be kept private and secure; thereby reducing the scope for personalisation. Alternatively, if we start diagnosing our illnesses accurately at home, the data caught to achieve this would dramatically widen the potential for personalisation. Most likely of all is that, as a global population, we will embrace and shun personalisation simultaneously. Which is pursued more fervently will, like a child eating two ice creams on a hot summer's day, switch according to taste and the perceived risks and benefits on offer.

A logical place to ground predictions for the future is in the emerging trends and technologies which promise to guide and influence future developments. Adopting this approach, there are currently three key technologies that will shape the use and adaptation of personalisation:

Content platforms - the ability of platforms to integrate with data will need to match the expected increase of visual, auditory and somatic interfaces where digital experiences are served.

Data capabilities - increased computing power and data processing capabilities will lead to automated real-time analysis, insight and activation across unrelated data points.

Sensors – a surge in the data points for each customer will be driven by biological, locational and other sensory inputs.

We can say with some confidence that these technologies will be hugely influential to the future of personalisation. However, it's now time to kiss goodbye to the safety of current trends.

It's time to stick our neck out. After all, it's near the end of the book and we need a climax. So here goes, we're going to imagine the future! (We would like to remind anyone reading this in 2025 or beyond, that we have made these predictions ourselves, with our unassisted, natural brain. That's genuine thinking, no AI - you should try it yourself before you start sniggering.)

THE SHORT TERM

We can expect online and offline data to play a greater role in both digital and physical experiences. The two spheres will merge ever more: you'll be guided in stores by augmented reality signs to products you viewed on your mobile hours or days earlier.

Website experiences will become more like dashboards or apps with the ability to quickly access the actions or information a user requires based upon individual preferences. If someone repeatedly makes the same error with the interface - always falls out of the conversion funnel or shows a preference for content displays such as image galleries - then key structural elements of that interface will adapt. Personalisation engines will link in with more website elements, way beyond the swapping of images, copy and calls to action. The code that makes up the digital interface will be linked up so that key structural elements change on the fly. This will include serving entirely different interfaces to different users such as personalised navigations and visual hierarchies.

The work of brands to execute their personalisation strategy will be eased by the adoption of systems that allow for automated content updates based upon real-time CRM and browsing data. The web experience will be fully customisable at a personal rather than a segmented level but the focus will be on smarter segmentation of users according to their stage in the customer journey, rather than one-on-one personalisation for all.

As users of services, we will notice more contextual outbound advertising that aligns with the placement. Ad placement will be designed with the context in mind including the creative tone. The insight will be based upon previous behaviour of the customer and other segmentation factors. For example, adverts on YouTube will not only be targeted based on the user's interest, but the creative will be crafted to both appeal to the target group and have the same visual language as the video itself. Increasingly we will move away from pre-roll adverts and towards a world where the adverts are part of the fabric of the digital experience.

The IoT will enable a network of tools and utilities that will be able to learn from each other. As such, individuals will develop a personalised ecosystem of physical things that carry their digital fingerprint. Operating systems of the IoT will be able to deliver co-ordinated digital, personal assistance on a physical scale. Garden tools will be synched and primed for use, property maintenance will be co-ordinated and batched. All according to personal usage habits.

It will be increasingly popular for niche businesses to set prices differently for categories of customer. Initially this will appear as an extension of the concept of an "offer" but the ability to charge users a price based upon personal or behavioural information will maximise the reach of a product and, of course, profits. Should this happen, can you imagine the consumer backlash against technology being used against them? And so, the personalisation-privacy debate will rage on.

AND BEYOND...

Karen in Marketing is an Artificial Intelligence "friend" who can provide on-the-fly analytics and insights into customer behaviour allowing for rapid iteration of personalisation and content strategies. Content published to a device or screen can be personalised on an individual, ad hoc basis. Cognitive systems like IBM's Watson or Google's DeepMind will be able to analyse and learn from customers' social media profiles, therefore enabling communications to be based upon sophisticated profiling. Watson will be able to tell as much about you from analysing your network of friends as from your personal information.

It will no longer just be content that's personalised but even the tone and accent adopted by a customer service agent. Trustingly familiar, just what you'd hope for or expect. The virtual teachers your children and grandchildren interact with at school look, sound and communicate with them according to their individual learning preferences. Beyond the classroom, your virtual lawyer, doctor, accountant and bank clerk will refine themselves to be the most agreeable to you. A transatlantic accent for pilots, Australian enunciation for your doctor, what would you like?

The descendent of Uber and the Google Smart Car will make itself ready, without any request, by recognising patterns you typically exhibit before going to work or, perhaps, today it's your sister's house. The seating, music, lighting, interior colours and patterns, interfaces and cabin temperature will all be personalised to you depending on factors such as the time of day and destination. All determined before you even open the car door.

A two tier system of paid and unpaid access to the internet will develop; the popularity of each will swing with evolving consumer attitudes and wealth. All the data on the free access is treated as "fair game" and is encouraged with the offer of cheaper prices; whilst the paid alternative allows for data ownership and co-monetisation between individuals and businesses.

Your new bionic knee knows that your shoes need replacing and instructs your 3D-printer to create a new pair for you, customised according to the exact locations of muscle tensions and weaknesses. Tech housed within our bodies will contribute to a nutritious, disease-preventative shopping list. Supermarkets add this data to your profile, combining it with information purchased from third parties and all the social data from every account you use. Specific insights extracted by any one of these personalisation facilitators will, with your approval, be instantly shared with your local council. Developing issues within a city or its population will be foreseen way in advance – and the local governments will do nothing, constrained by the budget cuts of the last great recession!

Personalisation will eek into every corner of our lives. The scale and depth of its insights will continually grow as we are able to include ever-increasing amounts of data from the public domain. It is perfectly conceivable that data collected by giants such as Google will be released after 70 years; revealing a historic gem of health information relating to an individual's ancestors.

As the youngest generation's digital media permeation reaches saturation, we might see a shift towards IRL (in real life) experiences. Service with a personal touch exemplifies a level of authenticity and sincerity beyond the algorithmic nature of a digital platform. The focus of businesses, particularly luxury brands, will be to refocus on a "real", personal, human-to-human interaction. Although data and computational capabilities will remain as active as ever in a background capacity with CRMs used to prompt warm-blooded, customer sales agents. And yet, however fashionable or desirable it may be to reduce individual and corporate reliance on technology; in the main, future generations will likely blend even more deeply with the computer systems around them. Biometric connections to the data will seize someone's attention or stimulate actions according to the optimum insight determined by the artificial intelligence feeding directly into their central nervous system, likely using blood implants. An incredible thought.

And what if we said you'll live to see this world? Many of you reading this in 2016 will.

(cue laughter from the class of 2062)

A personalisation recipe for brands

In short, you are going to need: data, insights, priorities, business goals and an objective view on the value of personalisation.

You also need people. Personalisation merges content and marketing teams directly with the technology. Data analysis, content production, marketing and technology capabilities all input into the solution. Although improvements in technology will continue to reduce human resource requirements, you still need everyone to be singing from the same hymn sheet. Five personas in three scenarios can mean fifteen variables instead of three. Workshops and documentation help to share key knowledge and set up workstreams. Proper planning also pays dividends. There needs to be ongoing commitment to the management and optimisation of content, including automation.

Below are steps to help brands deal with the five most common challenges with executing personalisation.

KNOWING WHAT TO PERSONALISE

1) Ask the customers
2) Take a data informed approach

3) Be led by user experience
4) Test and learn

HOW TO DEFINE THE PERSONALISATION PROGRAM OF WORK

1) Formalize business objectives of personalisation and the project goals
2) Identify common customer journeys beyond digital touch points
3) Map the key digital user journeys
4) Identify behavioural personas
5) Identify personalisation executions for those personas
6) Define the triggers that mean a user is treated as a persona
7) Identify data, analytics, content and tech requirements for each execution
8) Evaluate against ROI and project objectives
9) Create a prioritized program of work with a backlog of activities

HOW TO RUN THE PERSONALISATION PROGRAM OF WORK

1) Get advice about the technology solution you intend to use and see demos of platform providers like

Adobe and Sitecore as well as smaller specialists like Optimizely.

2) Define all the personalisation work in a matrix that is agreed by stakeholders
3) Organise content using a digital asset management tool
4) Optimise content using A/B tests
5) Have good project governance
6) See what works and iterate

HOW TO MAKE THE MOST OF DATA

1) Audit all the platforms to see what data is being collected
2) Sort the data into categories or buckets
3) Merge and analyse multiple datasets
4) Map the data to customer journeys
5) Focus on data relating to the important stages of the most important journeys

HOW TO HANDLE PRIVACY CONCERNS

1) Have a clear privacy statement that details your policies
2) Only collect the data you are going to use
3) Audit and have a policy specifically for personal information

There are frequently new innovations in online privacy. The Electronic Privacy Information Centre (epic.org) keep a directory of useful tools. Currently it is incumbent on the individual to take action to maintain their privacy. It is very complacent, dangerous even, to not read terms and conditions on the assumption that organisations and governments are acting in your best interests. They aren't. This may soon change but in the meantime:

FIVE THINGS YOU CAN DO IN FIVE MINUTES

1) Manage your social media privacy settings. They are usually found under "My Account"
2) Review the app permissions on your smart phone. In particular look out for those where you're sharing your location and contacts data without really needing to
3) Use the anonymous search engine duckduckgo.com
4) Use a private browser or regularly clear the cookies from your normal browser
5) Remove and never use public wifi from your phone

Glossary

AI is the intelligence exhibited by machines or computers

Analytics involves the tracking, measuring and querying of data

Archetypes represent certain identifiable characteristics in real people that exist

Behavioural describes characteristics relating to the needs and patterns of people's behaviour

CMS is a Content Management System from which digital content can be managed, edited and published

Cookies are dropped on people's browsers as they surf the internet and can be used for registering and recalling online actions

Cohorts represent a group of people with a shared characteristic

Customer Journey Maps describe routes of touch points within a customer's experience

CRM is a Customer Relationship Manager for storing and managing information about a customer

CTA is a Call to Action which draws attention to an action users are persuaded to take on a digital platform

DAM is a Data Asset Manager for cataloguing, storing and distributing digital assets

Data Buckets are ways of grouping categories or types of data

Data Warehouse is for storing and managing data from multiple data sources

Data Protection is the governance of how data should be handled

Demographic describes characteristics relating to the structure of populations

Dynamic Content is digital content that changes based upon given criteria such as user interactions

EDM is electronic direct marketing which involves brands communicating with customers by email

Hype Cycle is a branded graphical representation of the maturity and social adoption of technology by Gartner

Insight is the capacity to gain an accurate and deep understanding of someone or something

IoT is the Internet of Things which describes a network of physical objects having internet connectivity

IP is an Internet Protocol address for assigning a numerical identified to each device participating in a computer network that uses the Internet

KPIs are Key Performance Indicators that measure the success of a given activity against criteria

Legacy Systems are computer systems or applications programs that are outdated

Omnichannel is in reference to a presence across all communications channels

Personas are fictional characters created to represent different user types

Psychographic describes characteristics relating to interests, attitudes and opinions

ROI is Return on Investment meaning the value that is accrued by virtue of an activity

Segments are groups of people defined as having common needs or interests

User Stories describe the touchpoints of a digital journey from the user's perspective

VR is an artificial environment experienced through sensory stimuli provided by a computer

Visual hierarchy is the arrangement or presentation of elements that implies relative importance

About R&D Griffith-Jones:

Two brothers, Rob and David, with 30 years' experience of working together, undefeated in 2-on-2 football and, now, co-authors of this book.

David is a digital strategist and Rob a copywriter. With minds that complement each other and many shared interests, we will continue to explore subjects that fascinate us.

In the meantime, keep in touch at:

@BobGriffJones

@DigitalDavidJ

www.ingramcontent.com/pod-product-compliance
Lightning Source LLC
Chambersburg PA
CBHW070330190526
45169CB00005B/1824